devotions
for ministry couples

Stan Toler
Linda Toler

wesleyan
publishing
house

Indianapolis, Indiana

Copyright © 2008 by Wesleyan Publishing House
Published by Wesleyan Publishing House
Indianapolis, Indiana 46250
Printed in the United States of America
ISBN: 978-0-89827-388-5

contents

Faith is deliberate confidence in the character of God whose ways you may not understand at the time.

—Oswald Chambers

M inistry life often means paradox, joyful and heartbreaking at the same time; motivating and discouraging; hopeful, yet full of despair. Where can couples find the courage to minister in the midst of such contradiction? Let courage flow from your faith in God.

He is the great I AM. Not some unknowable higher power, but the God who reveals himself; the God who created, loved, and redeemed us; the God who brought you together as a couple and called you to minister in this particular time and place.

God is the very essence of good, and he authors the life story of every ministry couple. You may not be able to explain right now how every event of your life expresses God's goodness and care for you; pain and suffering cause real hurt, even when you're in ministry. Still, you can trust that God has your best interests at heart even when you don't understand.

So, have faith when your words are twisted by others. Believe when your plans are derailed. Trust when you don't know where the moving boxes are going next. God is faithful, and he will complete the good work he is doing in you.

One day, you may have the privilege of seeing some of the story lines converge, of understanding a deeper significance behind the inconveniences, challenges, and tragedies you experience. Or, like Job, you may not. Either way, know that God is good, and that he is writing a wonderful story of grace and redemption in the lives of you and your spouse.

faith into action

Name the circumstance that most threatens your faith today. Then express to God your trust in him regarding that situation.

paRadox
courage
Flow
twisted
derailed

Fix in us Thy humble dwelling;
all Thy faithful mercies crown.
—Charles Wesley

Have you ever taken a spiritual gifts inventory? If so, you've probably taken more than one. And if you're like many others in ministry, you've probably been amazed at the apparent disconnect between the gifts the inventory identified and your niche of service. Perhaps they don't appear to match.

Why is that?

Doesn't God give to each of us the abilities we need to fill our role? Doesn't he oversee the details of our lives, including where we are called to serve? Why would he send us to a place where those particular talents are not understood or appreciated?

God knows that if we fit effortlessly into our place of service, there will be no polishing of our faith. Our gifts need to be pounded and chiseled by the hammer of ministry. We need our rough edges smoothed by the honing that comes from working with challenging circumstances and difficult people. God's gifts are perfect, but remember that they come in human packages. Real-world ministry gives those gifts the gleam they need to shine for his glory.

Then God asks us to exercise a little creativity of our own. Rather than simply doing what we've always done, we sometimes need to reexamine the abilities we've been given and find a creative way to use them where we're currently serving. Take a fresh look at your ministry circumstances and ask God to help you see new possibilities for using your gifts through the power of his Holy Spirit.

faith into action

Ask your spouse to identify the spiritual gifts you are utilizing in your ministry setting.

Wherever you are—
be all there.
—Jim Elliot

Details of ministry life swarm around us like mosquitoes. Their reminders dot our refrigerator doors and pop up in our electronic organizers. Usually it's no problem to remember big priorities; it's the minutiae of ministry that sneak up to bite us. Yet, attentiveness to the small things will carry you a long way.

Individual words, thoughts, and attitudes matter. Not only do they shape others' opinions of us, they also help to shape who we are and what we're becoming in Christ. Carelessness in these areas causes spiritual lethargy. It will also hinder your ministry to others. But when we pay attention to such details

> Be shepherds of God's flock that is under your care.
> —1 Peter 5:2

in our private and public lives, we give credence to the grace that is in our souls.

Be attentive also to the concerns and feelings offered by parishioners. They might seem trivial when compared to the broader scope of church life, but you can be sure that they're a big deal to the person who took the time to share them. Church members who share personal details about their lives are offering you a window into their souls. They're also extending you a compliment, indicating their belief that you care about them as people, not just numbers. Honor their confidence in you by listening and being attentive. You'll probably learn something that will help you more capably minister to them as whole persons.

The genius of an effective ministry is in the details. When the fireworks of special days and events have fizzled, people remember and appreciate those who show genuine interest in their lives. Pray for God's help in being attentive to the small things, like managing your thoughts, attitudes, and personal interactions.

faith into action

Identify three parishioners that haven't received your personal attention in a while. Contact them to ask if there is anything you can pray about with them.

Happiness is a perfume you cannot
pour on others without getting
a few drops on yourself.

—Ralph Waldo Emerson

L ive together joyfully. Sounds like a happy assignment, doesn't
it? Add the pressures of ministry and everyday life, and it
might sound more like a chore. How do you do it?

Tell Stories. Capture and retell the stories of God's blessing
in your ministry together—when he transformed a person's life,
when you received a meaningful note of affirmation, when
a person you equipped took over a key ministry position.
Celebrating God's blessings regularly will strengthen your
enjoyment of life as a ministry couple.

Take a Break. Having regular times of recreation together will enhance your relationship and strengthen your ministry. Take up a sport together. Go shopping together. Take a nightly walk together. Note the key word: *together*. Find a hobby you both enjoy and go for it.

Relax. Ministry is stressful. Build time into your schedule to relax together. Maybe you'll invest in a couple of rocking chairs and put them on the front porch with a table to hold a tall glass of iced tea or lemonade. Spend some time just being quiet together at the end of a day.

Be Romantic. Nothing multiplies the happy endorphins like love. Make romance and affection a part of every day in your home. Smiling at your spouse across the room or writing a short love note gives you a boost; being the recipient feels awesome too. Invest in your marriage. It will be there when your last parish is just a memory.

faith into action

Plan time together away from the ministry routine. Look at your calendar and make it a date.

There should be a window toward
the sky in every house.

—Author Unknown

You were born into different families. You attended different schools. You were blessed with different gifts. But you share the same love.

One of the first blessings God gave your ministry was to bring the two of you together in a marriage that would become the foundation for your life of service. Your marriage, no matter what shape it's in at the moment, is a gift for which you can thank God.

Being thankful for your partner is one of the more useful marriage skills for any couple. For a ministry couple, it is crucial.

More than most, your relationship will experience significant wear and tear. There is stress. There is fatigue. There is demand. You have to project optimism when you feel negative. You're required to serve when you want to relax. You must be open to the demands and criticism of others, yet find the emotional resources you need to keep giving.

Few people can understand the stress that you experience in ministry as well as your spouse. No one is better suited to walk the path with you than your mate. No one else knows where you've been and where you're going. What a rich gift is the person whose life is so entwined with yours!

Nurture thankfulness for your spouse. Let it begin with a prayer today. Begin every morning with a routine like this one. As your feet hit the floor, say to God, "Father, thank you for this day that you have made, and thank you for the gifts my spouse brings to our marriage." Then list a new gift each day. If you think carefully, it will take several days to list each gift. Then you can start all over again.

faith into action

Recall a meaningful word of praise someone gave your spouse recently and repeat it to him or her today.

To be happy at home is the
ultimate result of all ambition.
—Samuel Johnson

I f ever a Scripture was used to justify a fight, it's Ephesians
4:15.

"But I'm just speaking the truth in love!"

Right! And was your intent to build up your partner or to
make yourself look or feel better?

Healthy relationships are based on truth. Without truth,
there is no trust. Without trust, there is no commitment. Without
commitment, there is no relationship.

The remarkable relationship we enjoy with our Heavenly
Father is possible because he is the God of truth. Actually, he

is truth. He knows the truth about who we are, including our fears and failures. He knows the truth about the plans he has for us. He invites us to come to him in truth, confessing our sins and weaknesses freely.

God designed human relationships so that they are governed by the same principle. Truth is the lifeblood of a marriage. There is no greater darkness than to discover that your spouse has lied to you. Perhaps it's because an untruth ruined the first earthly relationship between Adam and Eve. Maybe that's why deceit is such a hideous betrayal. We know its history.

There's good news for the guilty, though. Truth shatters the walls built by lies. It takes a little time to clear the debris, but a commitment to truth will help to restore the precious joy that's found when you trust your spouse in areas such as financial issues, sexual struggles, and emotional needs.

But when you speak the truth, don't forget to speak it in love. It's all too easy to speak the truth *to* someone you love without speaking it *in* love. As you communicate with your spouse, remember to speak with humility, understanding, compassion, and sensitivity.

faith into action

Be vulnerable and share something with your spouse that you've never shared before.

Sweet is the smile of home;
the mutual look when hearts
are of each other sure.
—John Keble

Tenderness is the gentle part of love. It's the hidden soft spot that resides in your inner heart. It's the glow you feel inside when you read a Hallmark card. It's the warmth you sense when you remember your wedding day. It is life's caress—the soul of relationships.

In the bright lights and bold design of an aggressive, in-your-face world, tenderness has the stark appeal of a black and white photograph. It brings to a marriage an element that is necessary and vital.

For wives, tenderness is often expressed as a kind of nurturing, an almost maternal emotion that causes her to stroke her husband's hair or baby him when she knows he really doesn't need it. For husbands, tenderness can be a type of adoring worship that makes him want to regard her as a princess—fragile and valuable.

Tenderness is not silliness, although neither does it exclude silliness. It is not giddy gushing or ridiculous expectations. It is the real-life emotion that we guard so carefully because it reveals so much about us. It may be as subtle as a glance, yet as powerful as a sermon.

Tenderness springs from the well of holiness. A heart surrendered is a heart fulfilled. Each couple must find their own way to express tenderness to each other. But it always begins with an attitude of respect and admiration. Refuse to suffer disdain and contempt. Never allow the uniqueness of your spouse to sabotage your adoration. Keep your spouse in the treasure chest of your heart. The key to the treasure chest is tenderness.

faith into action

Find the right time and place in the busyness of your day to write or speak a tender word to your spouse.

Help me to watch and pray;
and on Thyself rely.
—Charles Wesley

A ministry couple is well-served by an attitude of patience. You have probably already experienced a lot together: setbacks, challenges, and difficulties. Patience will ensure that you finish the race you started together.

Many people confuse patience with what the Bible calls *longsuffering*—being able to put up with inconvenience and irritation. That's pretty important. But patience, as Paul uses it in the verse above, has more to do with perseverance, diligence, and steady persistence.

So that you may have great endurance and patience.

—Colossians 1:11

No person in ministry would tell you that it is a cushy vocation, even with a plush chair in your office. Ministry embraces difficulty. Even the name—*ministry*—implies it. People that need ministry have a need or a problem or a challenge. They have a hurdle to overcome either as an individual or as a group. Bearing up under these situations requires patience. So does ministering to people facing such circumstances.

Ministry defies short-term gratification. How do you tell whether your teachings on spiritual virtues are sinking into the minds and heart of your parishioners? How are you to know if the couple you counsel will stay together? You don't. Sometimes you don't know for a long time. That's where patience comes in.

Ministry exacts a toll on the pastor's marriage too. You have to give your spouse the room to continually grow to meet the demands of ministry. You have to believe in each other and in your journey together. Patience makes this possible.

Patience is made more perfect by tribulation. Ministry offers frequent self-tests on patience. The grade matters, but the real test is whether you keep doing your homework.

faith into action

Take five minutes to reflect on a time of testing in your past and what you learned from it.

The wise man will seek to acquire the
best possible knowledge about events,
but always without becoming
dependent upon this knowledge.
—Dietrich Bonhoeffer

Ministry couples need wisdom. Seminary knowledge will guide you through the mechanics of ministry, but wisdom will hold you steady as you navigate the choppy waters of leadership and parish relationships. How is wisdom gained?

By Getting Close to God. Listen for God's voice during your quiet time, but don't stop there. See him in the world, at work in the details of life. Acknowledge his presence. Talk to him. Let his smile play on your face. Be enveloped by his grace.

By Learning From Others. Reading a book or consulting with a mentor, learn from the wisdom of others. By gaining insight from those who have walked a similar road, you'll avoid pitfalls and find the best routes on your ministry journey. Pay attention to others' criticism. There is often at least a kernel of truth to be discovered in their comments.

By Widening Your Scope. There are many perspectives on any given topic or situation. Having the maturity to explore the facts and research other views is healthy and makes your decisions more meaningful. It's tough to listen to opposing opinions, but it's good discipline.

By Living Your Life. Some wisdom can only be gained by experience. That's one of the reasons the Proverbs say we are to honor those with gray hair—they have endured and grown stronger. We need to follow suit. Life will continually teach us if we are willing to listen. As Benjamin Franklin said, "The doors of wisdom are never shut."

faith into action

Go to a Christian bookstore or library and select a book to help you gain wisdom about an area of your ministry.

A kind heart is a fountain of
gladness, making everything
in its vicinity freshen into smiles.

—Washington Irving

There's a surefire way to detect a person's attitude—listen to what comes out of his mouth. Words are the proof of the perspective. For ministry couples, attitudes can quickly become a destructive force in their relationship.

With the deluge of issues confronting a husband and wife in ministry, it's easy and natural to unload everything on the closest living human—your spouse. In the office and on the phone, you must remain polite, compassionate, calm, and composed. In the haven of the parsonage, you feel safe to pour out all the stresses you've had to deal with during the day. Tolerance for parishioners or patience with the kids is exchanged for irritation with your spouse.

What do we do about it?

Awareness of the problem is the key. We know that our husband or wife should not have to bear the brunt of our personal problems. In our more sane moments, we agree on this. But on those insane days when our attitude is an issue, it's difficult to snatch even ten minutes together, let alone calmly discuss what each is experiencing in the church and home. So, it's important to have a plan.

Make the personal decision: "I will not take out my stress on my spouse through my words and attitude." Write it on a note card and put it with your Bible or devotional book. Read it everyday (and sometimes every hour!). A lifestyle of holiness expresses itself in a kindness that comes from, and looks like, Christ.

faith into action

Find a healthy outlet for your ministry frustration and anxiety so that it doesn't poison your relationship with your spouse.

It is not how much we have,
but how much we enjoy,
that makes happiness.
—Charles Haddon Spurgeon

When you compare your lives to others, it's easy to become envious. A high school friend is now a successful businessperson. A board member at your church just purchased a summer home in an exclusive resort area. Even your friends in ministry all seem to have landed in bigger, wealthier, more successful churches. No wonder the patch of pitiful weeds under our feet seems a much paler shade of green than the lush carpet of grass we see all around us.

If envy is the enemy of contentment, how can we drive out jealousy and learn to be satisfied with our current circumstances?

Be content with
what you have.
—Hebrews 13:5

"Seek first the kingdom of God and his righteousness" (Matt. 6:33). Remember that you signed on to help Jesus accomplish a mission and accepted his assignment. The successful completion of any worthwhile mission requires focus and sacrifice.

Remember too that God has a plan for your life. It might not make sense to you at the moment, but one day looking back, you'll be grateful for the careful guidance of a God who sees everything so much more clearly than you do.

If you are in a toxic ministry situation that is destroying your family, contentment is not the answer. You need to get some help or get away. More often than not, though, the enemy of contentment is self-centered desire. Fight with all your mind and heart to take jealousy captive rather than let it capture you. Focus on the kingdom, and everything you need will be provided for you.

faith into action

Walk around your house or office and see it through the eyes of contentment.

Breathe on me breath of God;
fill me with life anew, that I may
love what Thou does love, and
do what Thou wouldst do.

—Edwin Hatch

Forgiveness is so difficult and so necessary. No marriage will survive the long haul unless both partners practice forgiveness. Those of us in ministry are still human. We make mistakes. Bad ones. Sometimes we neglect our partners. Sometimes we hurt each other. We need forgiveness. Not just today, but many days.

Ministry couples are more than marriage partners; we are also ministry partners. We rely on each other in two different arenas—private and public. When one of us disappoints the other, shutting down is not a good option. If one partner shuts down, not only does it affect private family relationships, it also impacts your public ministry. And when it comes to ministry, every pastor understands the pressure of knowing that "the show must go on." The answer, though far from simple, is to seek understanding and forgiveness.

True, you may have an appointment in fifteen minutes and the discussion has to wait, but it's important to deal with the issue later, rather than hoping it will go away. You ignore it at your own peril.

Instead, try the following. Wait for a neutral time and setting. Take the initiative in explaining how the conflict affected you; then try to understand how the conflict affected your spouse. Together identify the true source of the conflict. Take it upon yourself to be the first to forgive, without preaching. Finally, discuss alternative actions or reactions to the situation.

A wise pastor's wife once said, "Never go to church angry with each other." It's a good practice. God won't bless an unforgiving spirit.

faith into action

Determine ahead of time that you will forgive your spouse for hurting you without exacting revenge.

Every believer is God's miracle.
—Phillip James Bailey

Too often, husbands and wives mentally categorize and label their mates. "You're so lazy!" When negative labels are verbalized, the spouse feels attacked and disrespected. Such comments strike below the surface, touching a person's self-worth. Now, the fighting is not over the issue at hand, but for the offended one to regain self-worth.

Maintaining respect is easier when you resist having negative thoughts about your spouse. Not that you need to see him or her as beyond reproach, but focus most on the positive, valuable aspects. No one, including you and your spouse, is free from faults or foibles. We can choose to dwell on those more negative aspects, or we can choose to view the person as created in God's image and worthy of our respect and admiration. If you want a healthy relationship, choose to admire your spouse.

Here are some tips to maintain an attitude of respect, even in the midst of a disagreement.

- Maintain eye contact.
- Don't walk out on your spouse.
- Never label your spouse by calling him or her stupid or useless.
- Learn to say, "I disagree, but I understand your viewpoint."
- Find a way to offer a genuine compliment.

See your spouse with a Christ-look. His created beings are perfect in his eyes, not only because of their possibility, but also because of his affection for them. A holy life can demand no other.

faith into action

Write down a list of twenty items that you respect about your spouse. If you can't think of twenty, either you're not thinking hard enough or you're begrudging respect.

If you will work *for* God, form
a committee. If you will work
with God, form a prayer group.
—Corrie Ten Boom

There is no denying the powerful undertow of life's frustrations and discouragements. Negativity slaps us in the face every morning; whether it's the morning paper, talk radio, or your favorite Internet news site. Commentators rehearse a litany of bad tidings: allegations, arrests, protests, sanctions, scandals, ultimatums, and attacks.

News at the congregation level may be just as discouraging: ineffective committee meetings, disagreements, sour relationships, antagonists, lack of ownership, and lack of commitment. Okay, enough of that. You get the picture.

Adam and Eve were probably the only ones to ever know what is was like to wake up to a brand new day filled solely with optimism and opportunity. Even they found a way to put a negative slant on life. They wondered why they didn't get to be like God. Ever since, we've had to contend with the constant, nagging pull of pessimism and disillusionment.

One of the best ways to love your spouse is to be his or her cheerleader. Cheerleaders know their team is flawed. They know the team won't win every game. They know that absolute, perfect plays almost never happen. Still, they cheer. Cheerleaders spotlight their team's spectacular moments and convince the crowd (and the players) that their team can be successful in spite of its imperfections. Spouses should do the same.

Counteract the onslaught of negativity that greets your mate every day and show your support in a way that says, "I think you're great." Cheerleading for the one you share your life with makes life's game so much more pleasurable. And knowing that you believe in him or her is one of the greatest motivators your loved one will ever experience.

faith into action

Write a short note of encouragement to your spouse. Leave it where he or she will find it at the beginning of the day.

Let me be your servant, let me
be as Christ to you; pray that
I may have the grace to let
you be my servant too.

—Richard Gillard

Generosity is a precious gift. Here are five generous gifts
you can afford to give.

Your Spouse's Time. Make couple time a priority, but learn
to tolerate the interruptions. When your spouse is pulled away
unexpectedly, don't punish him or her. Understand that it goes
with the territory. Your arms are the still the ones your spouse
will relax in, and your ears are the ones that will hear his or
her most private thoughts.

Your Spouse's Energy. Ministry is a fast-paced, high-energy
lifestyle. At the end of the day, you're both probably drained of

emotional and spiritual resources. Your kindness and compassion, demonstrated in word and deed, can re-energize a tired soul.

Your Spouse's Interests. You might not share all interests, but you can always show interest. Give your partner the space to participate in an activity he or she enjoys without fear of resentment.

Affirming Your Spouse. Words cost little, but they can build stronger marriages. Just as you need your heavenly Father's affirmation spiritually, your spouse needs your affirmation emotionally. Never be afraid you'll praise your spouse too much. You can't be too generous.

Showing Affection for Your Spouse. Tender touches and romantic overtures are the language of love. Each couple must decide for themselves how to show affection for each other, but the key is to be generous in your affection for your partner. Leave no doubt about your love.

When you give of yourself generously, you receive from others generously. Jesus said, "With the measure you use, it will be measured to you" (Luke 6:38).

faith into action

Discuss with your spouse what kind of generosity is most meaningful to each of you.

Lord, take my life and make
it wholly Thine; fill my poor
heart with Thy great love divine.

—J. Edwin Orr

Holiness isn't displayed by what it gains but by what it gives.

You signed up for sacrifice at the altar on your wedding day. Which is where, of course, sacrifices take place. Yours is not a visual, dramatic scene of sacrifice, but a deep, continuing, life-long process.

Sacrifice means I give up something that is mine for someone else. Marriage alone gives a couple many reasons to sacrifice for the other; ministry adds an even greater dimension.

The Creator built sacrifice into the equation of love and then demonstrated it in his own plan of redemption. His Son was eternity's future laid on the altar. The Father loved the world and expressed it by sacrifice.

We must follow the divine example. Love that is not underwritten by sacrifice is too cheap to trust. When we lay down our own pride, reputation, wishes, viewpoints, and preferences in deference for our spouse, we prove the depth of our love and commitment.

Sacrifice sounds noble in words, but it is usually quite messy in reality. The sacrifices of the Old Testament were smelly, bloody affairs. You don't slaughter a large animal and pour its blood onto the altar and keep everything tidy. But this transaction wasn't for looks. It was for pardon.

The sacrifices we make for the one we love are not without difficulty. Sacrifice involves denying self—and that is always a cumbersome activity. But the prize of relationship is worth the cost. Take out your wedding pictures to remember why.

faith into action

Take a moment to consider the many sacrifices your spouse has made for your sake. Thank God for your husband or wife, then express your gratitude to your spouse.

There is no more lovely, friendly and
charming relationship, communion
or company than a good marriage.

—Martin Luther

E yes. Ears. Socks. Shoes. Salt and pepper shakers. They all
come in pairs.

While not every person has a mate, people have always
worked best in pairs too. God could have given the first human
the capacity to reproduce all alone. He could have designed
him to be self-sufficient, with no need to depend on others.

But he didn't. God designed the human psyche with the
need for a mate, a companion. Even in his pre-fall state, the
first man felt loneliness. He was incomplete. Both male and
female were required to fully represent God's image. And

thus, the need for human companionship was born.

It is true that people can find happiness as a single adult. Many, perhaps including the apostle Paul, have proven it to be true. But still, no one could argue that we are made for singleness. God created us so that we naturally desire a companion—a mate for life.

Perhaps no other sport relies on companionship more than rock climbing. Climbers usually work in pairs—the lead person is called the *climber*, the second person is the *belayer*. The belayer feeds rope to the lead climber through a belay device which acts as a fiction brake. Should the lead climber slip, the belayer can activate the break and stop the climber's fall.

Think of the rocks you have scaled as a couple. Remember the times when your climbing partner prevented your fall? Long before people started challenging rock formations, the Creator put together the ultimate climbing team—one man and one woman facing the summit of life together. What an idea!

faith into action

Do something for the sake of companionship this evening, even if it's only a walk.

Christ is the head of this house, the unseen Guest at every meal, the silent listener to every conversation.

—Author Unknown

Submission has a bad rap. Too many people who don't know enough about it have tried to explain it. The Bible has the answer. No surprise there, since it was God's idea.

The idea in a nutshell: each spouse has a unique and essential role. The husband provides spiritual leadership for the home and family, and the wife supports the husband's decisions and assists him in nurturing the family.

The Scriptures give the specific manner in which a woman shows her love for her husband—by honoring his Spirit-led wishes, trusting his Spirit-given abilities, and recognizing his

Submit to one
another out of
reverence for
Christ.
—Ephesians 5:21

Spirit-anointed skills. Sometimes this is accomplished with ease; at other times, it requires a disciplined acquiescence. God's purpose is for good.

In likening the husband to Christ, God lays out an example that calls the man to a higher level of behavior. It is taken for granted that he will be a tender leader, remembering that the one in his charge is of great value, and he is answerable to God for his actions.

Submission is voluntary, purposeful surrender. Both spouses recognize their roles and their challenges. Neither is concerned about proving who is better. Each responds to his or her own job description, fulfills the needs of the other, and completes God's plan.

The best argument for submission is the one the Bible uses—Christ submitted himself to the will of the Father. Christ is God, equal with God the Father, yet obedient to him in the great plan of heaven.

faith into action

Discuss with your spouse what healthy, mutual submission looks like.

Grace is free, but when once you
take it you are bound forever to
the Giver, and bound to catch
the Spirit of the Giver.

—E. Stanley Jones

Servants serve. They're not surprised when others depend on them and that there are interruptions in their day. They are accustomed to being called upon to come to another's aid.

What distinguishes the servanthood of Christ is that he chose it. He saw the royal robes available to him and he chose the serving towel. Not only did he drape himself in humility when he washed the disciples' feet, but his very human life was evidence that he was, though Lord and Master, a servant of all.

We are called to do the same. How can a ministry couple serve each other?

- Help the other with ministry preparation when appropriate.
- Make sure the behind-the-scenes stuff gets done.
- Encourage the other to accept a new opportunity to use personal gifts.
- Provide a listening ear and caring attitude for the other.
- Practice the old fashioned art of being longsuffering.

The best servants are those who perform their tasks willingly, without grudging. A servant with a bad attitude always manages to spoil the work, even if the job itself is performed flawlessly. The truth of the matter is that we are called to serve, not because we thought of it, but because Christ did.

faith into action

Do something behind-the-scenes for your spouse.

Of all music that reached farthest
into heaven, it is the beating of
a loving heart.
—Henry Ward Beecher

t's just the two of you.

Especially for a ministry couple, having a fabulous secret that is shared only by two is special indeed. Virtually your whole life is lived in a glass house. The bedroom is the one place where the two of you are veiled from the gaze of outsiders. It is a sacred chamber of love, a pure and holy place—a rich gift from a loving Father.

It is paramount that a husband and wife who are engaged in ministry make efforts to fan the flames of their romantic relationship. Master the art of unobtrusive flirting with your spouse. Send romantic e-mail or text messages. Plan a romantic overnight or weekend getaway. Read a respectable book on sexual intimacy. Seek Christian counseling for sexual issues in your marriage. Keep your sexual relationship fun and imaginative. Above all, adore your spouse.

Our culture is slathered in suggestive images—the mall, the Internet, magazines, catalogues, even on the street. It uses sexual attraction inappropriately. Use your sexual attraction appropriately. The stress of ministry, the danger of emotional or physical affairs, and the risk of burnout—all are factors that have the potential to threaten your marriage covenant.

Guard your heart. Sex is a physical expression of your emotional and spiritual love. It is honorable in God's eyes. You bring honor to him as you give and receive love within your marriage.

faith into action

When's the last time you enjoyed a romantic getaway? Start planning (or at least dreaming about) your next one today!

Gratitude is the fairest blossom
which springs from the soul.
—Henry Ward Beecher

Gratitude will protect your ministry from the hot flames of bitterness. You may have noticed that there are occasional downsides to being in ministry. Gratitude, however, calls us to focus on the positives.

While there are challenges, there are also blessings. While the schedule stays pretty full, we have a more flexible schedule than most. Our parishioners may call us at inconvenient times, but they also write encouraging notes. Our family is under scrutiny, but we also receive sincere praise. Our budget is somewhat tight, but we also experience God's provision in remarkable ways.

> God . . . richly provides us with everything for our enjoyment.
> —1 Timothy 6:17

God gives to us richly. That is a fact. Gratitude is simply acknowledging the truth of it. When a husband and wife do not give mental assent to the things they have been given, they will remain poor, no matter how much more they receive. There is no lack like the absence of gratefulness.

Ungratefulness is as contagious as a cold. When one person has it, it usually spreads to another. But when gratitude fills the heart and home, richness resides within. We've learned how to count our blessings and give off the top. No matter where we've been on the economic scale, there has always been a bright, God-blessed side. We never know what it will be, or where it will come from. But at just the right moment, our faithful heavenly Father gives us an eye-opener so that we can see his abundant supply.

faith into action

Express gratitude for your ministry in the presence of your family.

Peace cannot be kept by force, it can
only be achieved by understanding.
—Albert Einstein

The key to marital peace is communication.

Most ministry couples would agree that the greatest enemy
of marital peace is conflict, and the most common source of
conflict is communication. True, some conflict occurs because
of differences in temperament and viewpoint, but the impact of
these can be greatly reduced by calm, rational communication.

Communication means more than mere conversing. It's
talking with a listening heart. It's delving into the intent and
thoughts of the other person. It's seeing beyond the words and
into the soul. Communication is frequently mentioned as one of

the vital components of a healthy relationship. There is good cause for it.

Communication says, what do you really mean by that? What hurt from the past is fueling your attitude? Help me understand why you feel so strongly about this. Or, I know if we just talk about this, we can come to a mutual understanding.

Many couples know the theory of good communication but find it difficult to put it into practice in the midst of conflict. Remember that communication is cumulative. How you respond today in a conversation with your spouse will affect how you respond tomorrow. The skills you employ today can be improved tomorrow.

Communication is about words, tone, eye contact, and body language. Study the art of all four. Learn to keep peace by assuming a manner that is non-threatening and a tone that is gentle. Taking your spouse's hand while discussing an issue may remind both of you that the person facing you is the one you love.

Relationships live or die as a result of the communication involved. Invest in yours with healthy communication.

faith into action

Practice the art of good communication with your spouse by choosing a hot topic and discussing the pros and cons.

> You cannot shake hands
> with a clenched fist.
>
> —Golda Meir

A husband once said that he and his wife never went to sleep angry with each other . . . but some nights they never went to bed. There has to be a better way!

In the Garden of Eden, conflict was foreign. But today, living, thinking adults have disagreements. Marriage is the arena where many of these dueling matches are staged. You can't prevent conflict from occurring in your marriage, but you can manage it. Keep proper perspective: it's only one disagreement, not the end-all of your life.

How you respond makes the difference. Avoid interrupting your spouse. Listen with your intellect, not just your emotions. Look for the facts in what the other is saying instead of pouncing on what you think you hear. Acknowledge that your spouse has the right to have a different viewpoint. Don't leave the room in anger; if you can't reach an understanding, arrange to discuss the issue later. In the meantime, act like it didn't happen.

> Do not let the sun go down while you are still angry.
> —Ephesians 4:26

Pray for gentleness and longsuffering. Couples in ministry struggle with relationships just like everyone else. Feeling excess guilt because you and your spouse had an argument right before the church service is wasted emotional energy. It's life. If, however, you were unkind to your husband or wife, you owe an apology and some loving words.

Be proactive. Expect normal conflict, and choose to prevent it from taking a toll on your relationship.

faith into action

Together, write a list of rules to observe during conflict.

Affection is responsible for
nine-tenths of whatever solid and
durable happiness there is in our lives.
—C. S. Lewis

Romance is the sparkle in living. And most ministry couples could use a little more sparkle in their routine. Romance is one of those non-vital, but enriching things in life. In other words, you can live without it, but it sure makes life a lot more pleasant if you have it.

A couple can share a home, raise a family, and partner in ministry successfully without having the added dimension of romance. It's extra trimming, to be sure, but it adds a lot of zing to living. Romance is not just about physical intimacy. It's not just about passion. It's more than affection. It's flirtatious, positive, complimentary—it's love with flair.

Traditional overtures of romantic feelings have been picnics and poetry, walks in the rain with a shared umbrella, and candlelit dinners. Symphony concerts, porch swings at night, and evenings by the fireplace are iconic venues for romance.

Romance is about whispers and long glances, seductive winks and slight caresses. It's the stuff of satin and moonlight, fragrance and roses. Yes, it's traditionally wives that dream about it, but husbands benefit as well. Men don't often wish specifically for romance, but when it's there, they enjoy the added shimmer it brings to their love life.

For a ministry couple, romance keeps a sweet secret alive that not only makes the marriage better, but enhances the ministry as well. Two happy people are much more productive in their work, especially if it's in church ministry.

faith into action

Buy some CDs or download some love songs. Play the music after dinner tonight.

The person who gets the farthest is generally the one who is willing to do and dare. The sure-thing boat never gets far from shore.

—Dale Carnegie

Every couple in ministry has goals, whether or not they have verbalized them. Some are more ambitious than others, and perhaps some are more appropriate than others. A healthy marriage and ministry seeks goals that honor God and builds his kingdom.

Goals are important because they help people make and measure their progress. Ministry operates on the principle of betterment—helping people achieve personal and spiritual improvement through the grace of God.

> Forgetting what is behind and straining toward what is ahead.
> —Philippians 3:13

Ministry couples can benefit from verbalizing and clarifying both their personal and professional goals. Putting into words those deep yearnings of the spirit helps to further their actualization.

Believe it or not, goal-setting makes for an awesome date. Set aside an evening or a weekend and dream together. Talk about what you want to accomplish together in your life and in your ministry. According to C. S. Lewis, "You are never too old to set another goal or to dream a new dream." Reach for the stars, daydream, and then put on paper the goals you want to work toward accomplishing.

Use questions like these to make your goals: Is there any level of education I still want to achieve? Where do we want to be financially at retirement? Is our present area of ministry a long-term position? What do we want our ministry to look like in five years? Ten years? What goals do we have for our children—educationally, emotionally, and spiritually? What is a dream that we would like to make happen?

Now, set milestones to help you achieve these goals—bite-size actions you can do on a daily, weekly, or monthly basis. Keep the list handy and review it regularly. It will help you stay focused.

faith into action

Set a date to dream about and plan your goals with your spouse.

God loves with a great love the
man whose heart is bursting
with a passion for the impossible.
—William Booth

Passion is focused fervor.

For the ministry couple, there is no substitute for such fervor
in life and ministry. Passion takes on many forms in everyday
living. It's a zest for living that converts to energy for personal
pursuits and happiness in dealings with others. It can be as
simple as a kind word or smile for the clerk, a motivating
comment to someone who is discouraged, or a pervading sense
of excitement about life.

Simple, but profound. Can people really live that way? Of
course they can. And they do! Too often we equate real life

with the way we're living now. To live life with passion, you have to break away from the mundane and the expected. Passion is intensity. Half-hearted attempts will not suffice.

The psalmist who wrote the verse above knew what he wanted from God, and he sought after it. So should we. Think of the passionate people described in the Bible. Moses, Joshua, Elijah, David, Esther, Ruth, Peter, Paul, Stephen, and Mary Magdalene were people who knew what they wanted from life as it pleased God—and were passionate about pursuing their goals.

There is a relentless undertow to life that constantly threatens to pull those in ministry under the waves of discouragement. Clutching onto passion for life and ministry will help you keep your head out of the water.

faith into action

Make a list of the twenty things that you are most passionate about. Then rank the top five.

O may all who come
behind us find us faithful.

—Jon Mohr

Grandchildren are one of life's sweet rewards. Grandparents love to give gifts to their grandkids. And the best gift a grandparent can give is an inheritance . . . a spiritual one.

You are investing in your grandchildren's inheritance every day. The decisions you make, the integrity you maintain, and the spiritual fervor you exhibit all form a spiritual heritage that you pass on to your grandchildren. Even if you presently do not have grandchildren, the investment you are making in your children's lives forms the foundation of the home they will someday have.

One of the bittersweet aspects of ministry involvement is that it often places distance between you and the ones you love. When you answer the call, you also accept the separation; but there is still the normal sadness that comes with the absence of chubby little hands holding yours, and sweet voices calling for Grandma or Grandpa.

You can turn a potential negative into a huge positive by being intentional about sharing a godly heritage with your grandchildren. Write letters to your grandchildren. Such handwritten notes are rare and precious today. In between letters, send e-mail or text messages. Be sure to plan special projects to do with them when you're all together again. Squeeze all the fun you can from the moments you have. The memories you make will last a lifetime.

Grandparents in ministry contribute richly to children's spiritual legacy. The example of service set before them will always have an impact on their relationship with Christ. And someday, you may reap the sweet blessing of watching your grandchild follow in your footsteps of service.

faith into action

Contact your child or grandchild today and tell them that they are special to you.

Character in a saint means the
disposition of Jesus Christ
persistently manifested.

—Andrew Murray

Character is a million dollar topic today. Is it necessary? Is it important? Does it matter personally, professionally, privately? God's Word has a settled answer—it does. Integrity or personal character, guides the upright.

People in ministry are well acquainted with the topic of personal character. We know about character references and regular character reports. We are aware of the ever-present news reports regarding the fall of prominent leaders. We may have even witnessed the unenviable collapse of colleagues who have compromised their character.

How can you guard your precious integrity?

Maintain Proper Boundaries. This includes setting guidelines for conduct and professional practice.

Create Checkpoints that Ensure Honesty. Such systems lay the groundwork for transparency.

Submit to Personal Accountability. Give someone you respect and trust the keys to your secret thoughts and actions.

Open Your Soul to the Scrutiny of the Word. The Bible will expose the truth.

Holiness of heart brings holiness of character. And holiness of character is the mark of Christ on your very soul. D. L. Moody wisely said, "Character is what a man is in the dark." Live your life above reproach so that your integrity will illuminate the darkness.

faith into action

Start the process of finding an accountability partner.

God provides resting places as well
as working places. Rest, then, and
be thankful when He brings you,
wearied, to a wayside well.

—Mrs. Charles E. Cowman

Hospitality is inconvenient. Even for people who love to have others in their home, there is hard work and added stress. But God commands us to practice the gracious art of hospitality.

The reason is that hospitality strikes at the root of the gospel. God is all about meeting needs — the greatest need being salvation. He shared what he had, his Son, with us. On a daily basis, he shares from the pantries of heaven with us. He asks that we do the same here on earth.

Hospitality takes on many forms: making time in our schedule to meet a parishioner for lunch, opening our home to host an after-church snack for the teens, or offering a place of rest to visiting missionaries. Hospitality is sharing what we have with a willing spirit.

Hospitality reaps rewards. The parishioner we take to lunch may make spiritual progress from our interest and prayers. The teens will benefit from fellowship in a wholesome environment. The visiting missionaries will provide our children with some positive role models in living color.

Beware that some people abuse hospitality. Take a reasonable approach to opening your home and family life to others so as not to put your family in jeopardy. On the other hand, we should never allow unwarranted fear to prevent us from offering a cup of cold water in Jesus' name. Remember, too, that though Jesus was the greatest servant ever, he did not serve nonstop. Instead, he often took time alone to rest and rejuvenate. We need the same.

Hospitality is one of the most concrete and practical ways that ministry couples can extend the welcome of Jesus to people in their congregations and communities.

faith into action

Discuss with your spouse how your family can practice hospitality.

We must live in the atmosphere of
the Spirit, high in the mountains of
vision, and there the appetite for the
bread of heaven will be strong.

—G. Campbell Morgan

We know what prayer is: spiritual warfare, intercession, supplication. But incense? Our prayers rise before God. We kneel, we sit, and we stand. But no matter how we pray, we are talking to him. And the words are not bound by the rocky coastlines of earth; they ascend into the reaches of space and spiral up to God. The stench of Sodom and Gomorrah assaulted the presence of his holiness, but the fragrance of our voices raised to him can grace his throne.

Couples in ministry have many occasions to pray. But it's often difficult to find opportunities to pray together. Our schedules are hectic. The demands are many. Emergencies arise. The most difficult obstacle may be that we struggle with being vulnerable enough to pray in our spouse's presence.

Here's a simple way to initiate a pattern of prayer in your marriage. Start small—five minutes or less. Find a comfortable posture, whether kneeling, sitting, or standing together. Consider holding hands. Then, take turns offering a brief prayer about whatever is on your heart. Don't feel you must confess extremely personal things in your spouse's presence. Just speak to God in a way that feels safe to you. Be sure to avoid the temptation to preach at your spouse through your prayer; that's not what prayer is for. Once you've gotten over the initial hurdle of praying together, talk about what time works best and stick to it.

It may feel uncomfortable at first; new things usually do. But after awhile, you will enjoy being in the presence of God together.

faith into action

Talk to your spouse about establishing a couple's prayer time.

Managing finances is a life skill that every family member will need to sharpen. You are their teacher. When you practice good money management, you will encourage it in others.

—Stan Toler

How a couple manages money has far-reaching effects, not only for the marriage, but also for the ministry.

Historically, those in ministry have not been numbered among the wealthy. Pew rental paid what meager wages the earliest minister received; circuit riders embraced a Spartan lifestyle, and there is, of course, the standing joke about "being as poor as a church mouse."

This perception has changed in the era of televangelism and megachurch campuses built by multi-million dollar organizations. Now, the uninformed often suspect or assume that the pastor is doing quite well with the money received in the offering each Sunday. While there are no doubts many pastors who do quite well financially—and come by it honestly—there are just as many or more who struggle to get by, not because of poor management, but because their congregations are struggling to get by.

Whether you and your spouse find yourselves receiving a healthy income or a meager one, how you handle your financial affairs is vital. Here are some practical thoughts:

- Use a budget;
- Pay your tithe;
- Start saving yesterday;
- Plan for vacations and seasonal expenses;
- Use credit cards only for emergencies and purchases to be paid off in thirty days;
- Never discuss money problems at night;
- Pray with your spouse for wisdom in managing your financial resources.

faith into action

Buy a good book on financial management. Read it and put it into practice.

As we grow old, the beauty
steals inward.

—Ralph Waldo Emerson

While the world worships youth, we're all in the process of aging. The process was set in motion from the very moment of birth. And while the aging that leads to normal maturation is perceived as good and welcome, the aging that puts us on the downward slope of the hill is a most unwelcome intruder.

We are conditioned by our culture to grasp for and prolong our youth, rather than welcoming the next stage of our lives. God's Word values every age. It promises that when you find yourself further along the journey than you realized, he will

> Even to your old age and gray hairs I am he, I am he who will sustain you.
> —Isaiah 46:4

sustain you. He will carry you. He will make the latter years as fruitful as the former.

The challenges of aging sometimes make ministry more difficult. You and your spouse may face limitations you've never experienced before. God's ongoing presence will enable you to work through the process of accepting change and finding a new normal.

Ministry couples often find it difficult to retire. Maybe that's because ministry is anchored more firmly in the soul than in the intellect. People retiring from other jobs may be able to reduce or eliminate the activities required for their profession effortlessly, but the soul of a minister is always sensitive to a hurting world.

Though the age of retirement is ever changing, moving into the next season God has planned for you is a glorious opportunity. Seize it with all your strength. Your experience has made you wise enough, and your enthusiasm will make you strong enough. Your best—and most influential—times of ministry are always in the now.

faith into action

Think about a ministry beyond retirement, even if you're still years away. Start planning.

I believe *the* most important
contribution a parent can make
to his child is to instill in him
a genuine faith in God.
—James Dobson

Growing up in ministry is a privilege and a risk. Children of ministry parents have unique opportunities to see God at work in people's lives. They participate in events that others don't and interact with godly role models. They receive a healthy dose of Scripture and prayer as a by-product of living in a ministry home. They're immersed in a unique worldview.

Ministry children are also at greater risk to become ministry casualties, sometimes feeling trapped, exposed, or neglected. There may be nothing that hurts a ministry couple more than to watch a son or daughter walk away from the faith. They

> I have no greater joy than to hear that my children are walking in the truth.
>
> —3 John 4

may repeatedly ask themselves what they could have done differently.

Parents make mistakes. We're human, after all. Some children stray, not because of anything the parents have done, but because they see how their parents have been treated in ministry. Ultimately, though, your children choose their own pathway in life. As a parent, you tend to their spiritual, emotional, intellectual, physical, and financial concerns the best you can, and they respond according to their free will.

Your values can be contagious—if practiced with a contagious and positive spirit. Walking in truth means that you walk in holiness, living in the light and love of Christ.

The apostle John verbalized the conviction of all godly parents—biological, adoptive, or spiritual: there is no greater thrill than to hear that your children are following truth. And that journey may be incremental. Spiritual sensitivity in your children should be celebrated and encouraged. God is at work in them, and you stand beside the road, cheering them on.

faith into action

Discuss the positive aspects of your ministry with your family.

Adoration is the lifting up of the
heart and mind to God, asking
nothing but to enjoy God's presence.
—The Book of Common Prayer

Worship is the pinnacle of our weekend ministry efforts. The word *worship* usually brings to mind an image of praise teams and choruses, uplifted hands, and large gatherings. But the heart of worship is none of these. It can be loud; it can be a whisper. It can shout for delight; it can weep silently for joy. Worship is the adoration of the soul.

A husband and wife in ministry can be a powerful force for promoting worship. The worship that the ministry couple feels and expresses melds together and flows to the congregation. But attaining a worshipful state of mind can prove to be one

> Come, let us bow down in worship.
> —Psalm 95:6

of our most challenging tasks. Real life gets in the way.

Did the priests who served the temple ever struggle to enter into a spirit of worship? Of course we don't know. But from the Scriptures, we know that they had elaborate preparations, both physical and spiritual. Serving before the atonement of Christ, their ministry required a flawless appearance, scrupulous cleanliness, and absolute inner purity if they wanted to escape death. Their worship was judged partly on their outward adherence to the law.

Christ came to fulfill the law. Listen to his words to the woman at Samaria. "Yet a time is coming and has now come when the true worshipers will worship the Father in spirit and truth, for they are the kind of worshipers the Father seeks" (John 4:23). The sacrifice of Christ made the difference in how we worship.

Genuine worship flows from hearts that are obedient. Praise flows from a genuine adoration of Christ. Quieting your heart, either early on the day of worship or on the night before, can help prepare your spirit for meaningful worship. Paying attention to your private worship will greatly enhance your public worship.

faith into action

Write your own psalm of worship to God.

Friendship is unnecessary, like philosophy,
like art . . . It has no survival value;
rather it is one of those things that
give value to survival.
—C. S. Lewis

Friends are a precious commodity for those in ministry. It used to be said that a ministry couple should not have friends within the congregation. While fewer people hold to that wisdom these days, there are still some useful points to draw from it.

Having close friends within your congregations can be a delicate situation, particularly if others see you as favoring one family over another. Resist having an exclusive circle of friends. Consider including prospects, as well as long-time members in your social circle. Use social times to strengthen relationships and invest in others.

As much as possible, avoid mixing church business with social times, and at all costs, avoid gossip. Never assume that your conversation will be held in confidence. A little discretion will go a long way.

Even if you choose to develop close friendships with congregation members, you also need ministry colleagues. Most often this means people who are ministering under similar circumstances in another congregation. Such friends understand the unique challenges that you experience and can provide support that most people in your congregation are unable to provide.

A ministry couple also needs long-term friends. No one can take the place of your college buddies or your childhood friends who knew you way back when. It pays to hang onto these friendships and make the effort to keep in touch occasionally. They represent a part of your life that most of your present associates know little about. The old friends knew you when you were still becoming the person you are today. They probably contributed to your growth and development in a number of ways. Such friends, once gone, are impossible to replace.

faith into action

Make the effort to reconnect with an old friend today.

A primary task of every leader
is to bring out the best in
those around them.
—Stan Toler

Being mentored is for smart people.

Those who think they know it all, actually do. They know all they will ever know, because they are not teachable. Those who will place themselves under the instruction of another are already at the head of the class. They realize that there is always more to learn and that others have valuable insight to give them.

As a couple in ministry, seek opportunities to be mentored by those who have walked the path ahead of you. Submit to the supervisory structure over you and seek to learn what you can from the process governing your ministry.

Mentoring can occur on a personal or professional level. Some mentoring is done on a more casual basis; some is more formal. Whatever opportunities you have, take the chance to pick the brains of the wise men and women around you. Listen to their counsel and learn from their rebuke, if given. Keeping your mouth shut and hearing some unpleasant advice is good for all of us now and then.

And, someday, you will have the opportunity to sit on the other side of the sofa and give a few gentle tips to those following you. It's a circle of knowledge—keep passing it on.

faith into action

Ask for advice and listen to the answer!

Home that our feet may
leave, but not our hearts.
—Author Unknown

A ministry home is often a center for change. Frequent moves and fluid schedules are contributing factors to the unsettled atmosphere that goes with being in ministry. It seems that today is never the same as yesterday, and tomorrow already looks different from today. In the midst of such uncertainty, traditions can keep the family grounded in their own identity.

Household traditions give the family pillars that provide stability. You can look at them and say, "This is who we are; this defines us." Traditions can be grand or humble, frequent or occasional. But they should be meaningful. Some ideas are:

- An expected meal on the weekly menu, such as pancakes every Saturday morning.
- A weekly night for family togetherness, like eating out or playing games.
- An annual event, such as a conference, church activity, or family camp.
- Special holiday celebrations, like lighting an advent candle or attending a Good Friday service.
- A familiar routine, such as enjoying the same snack every Sunday night.

Traditions need not be elaborate or especially unique to be meaningful. The point is to give your family something all its own, common threads that establish your family identity. Such traditions can provide your family with a sense of community and your family members with much-needed emotional stability.

God uses the commonplace to beautify our lives and provide security. He made everything beautiful in its time. God uses the commonplace, such as the seasons, to remind us of constancy in the midst of our fluidity.

faith into action

Choose a simple tradition and begin implementing it this week.

He leadeth me! O blessed
thought! O words with
heav'nly comfort frought.

—Joseph H. Gilmore

The prayer for guidance is one of the most common prayers among all Christians, and especially among ministry couples. Such prayers can be especially urgent when responsibility feels like a two-ton weight, or when you're faced with a dilemma for which there is no good, apparent solution.

When you request guidance, you admit that you need help finding your way. There are many situations in which a ministry couple might feel this way, such as when making decisions about worship style, building projects, additional services, or transitioning to a different parish.

There are countless times when we crave guidance. The good news is that the Bible promises that God will always be there to guide us. Every believer, by God's Spirit, comes equipped with spiritual GPS.

1. God uses our intuition, working at times through thoughts and impressions.
2. God uses our gifts, giving us the wisdom to discern the right path.
3. God uses our spouse, speaking to us through the person he's placed in our inner circle.
4. God uses his Word, which never goes out of style and never stops being relevant to our daily lives.

We sometimes rely too much on a spiritual feeling, when maybe God wants us to pray and then take action based on the resources we have at hand. Granted, there are times when extended prayer is in order. But often, he has already given us all the guidance we need. It's there. We just need to look for it.

faith into action

Journal your next prayer for guidance and the answer you receive.

> The real democratic idea is, not that every
> man shall be on a level with every other,
> but that every one shall have liberty, without
> hindrance, to be what God made him.
>
> —Henry Ward Beecher

Ministry operates on the principle of authority. Success in ministry depends in part on how well you exercise, share, and interact with authority. You, as a ministry couple, exercise authority within a congregation or other group. You also may empower some of those you lead to exercise authority within a certain ministry of the congregation. On the other hand, you yourself are under the authority of your superiors, and ultimately of Jesus Christ. If this authority structure is not respected, the congregation will be hindered in its effectiveness.

As a couple in ministry, there will always be someone in authority over you—a district or conference leader, a board, or a committee. It demonstrates maturity of character and a proper perspective on your role as a ministry couple when you accept the authority of those under whom you serve. You'll be more likely to finish the campaign successfully if you respectfully salute the commanding body and diligently march in the direction advised.

As a leader, you'll also be called on to exercise your authority. Here is where the true test of a person's mettle is revealed. Will you use your authority to evade the unpleasant aspects of ministry, shoving them onto someone else? Or will you practice servant leadership, treating others as you would want to be treated?

Effective leadership is respectful leadership. The person who takes advantage of leadership and "lords it over" those who are being led will not be long for leadership. God will bless the leadership of those who focus on accomplishing the mission while treating each team member with understanding and respect.

faith into action

Read Romans 13 and discuss what it teaches about authority and submission to authority.

And tho' this world, with devils filled,
should threaten to undo us, we will
not fear, for God hath willed His
truth to triumph through us.
—Martin Luther

If challenges were bricks, a ministry couple could pave their walk with them. To minister is to face challenges. There are challenges with leadership, spiritual development, relationships, administration, teamwork, recruitment, time, and schedule, among other things.

Challenges are stressful, no doubt about it. Whatever the issue, challenges require an extra measure of confidence, courage, wisdom, energy, and stamina. But challenges can also be beneficial. They keep you focused on God's strength. They improve your game. They give you appreciation for the peaceful times. And they often represent great opportunity.

Husbands and wives approach challenges differently. While a man may want to gather the facts and seclude himself to come up with a solution, the woman often wants to discuss the situation and verbalize the options together. As you work together in ministry, it can be an additional challenge just to agree on how to wrestle with a challenge!

It's important to keep in mind that no challenge you face has surprised God, and your current situation will almost certainly not tell the final story of your ministry. With God there is calm assurance and a bright future. Spurgeon said, "Trials teach us what we are; they dig up the soil, and let us see what we are made of."

For every storm at sea, God is the life preserver.

faith into action

Recount a previous challenge and how God helped you through it.

Let parents bequeath to their children
not riches, but the spirit of reverence.
—Plato

E very parent gives a child a gift. Some parents give little more
than life. Others at least try to provide basic teaching and
guidance for living. Still others bless their children by passing
on a legacy of love and faith. Whatever you received from
your parents, whether great or small, remember to honor it
appropriately. Many adults harbor bitterness toward their father
or mother. In the end their bitterness brings them no profit.

Sure, parents are sometimes guilty of caring too much. If
yours are overstepping the boundaries, it's probably an oversight
and not intended to harm. Watching your child battle the seas

Listen . . . to your
father's instruction
and do not forsake
your mother's
teaching.
—Proverbs 1:8

of ministry can be very trying for a parent. As much as possible, extend mercy and grace.

As your parents grow older, one of the best ways that you can honor them is to provide for their care in whatever way you are able. Life expectancy rates are getting longer and more people are living into their 80's and 90's. For the ministry couple, caring for an aging parent adds a new level of stress to the mix. If you find yourself in these circumstances you might consider the following: discussing caregiving options with your siblings or other family members; examining various options for their long-term care; consulting an attorney and financial planner about their money management; and encouraging your parents to write a will and appoint an executor of their estate.

While you might think of caring for an aged person primarily as giving (and it is a sacrifice), people are often surprised by the feeling that they receive far more than they give—even as they care for their parents in the last days.

faith into action

Honor your mother and father, whether living or deceased, in a special way today.

In every conceivable manner,
the family is the link to our past,
and the bridge to our future.

—Alex Haley

Unfortunately, the word *in-law* causes many people to cringe. When we think of in-laws, we typically think of people who are not like us. It's a fact that opposites attract. Your spouse is different because he or she comes from a different family with its own unique history, personality, culture, and quirks.

Sometimes people have conflict with their in-laws because their families have little common background. It's a person who brings them together, a person who often feels caught between the people he or she loves.

This natural contention can be intensified if either or both sets of parents are also involved in ministry. The grind of mutual ministries can wear on the relationship. Experience is often a better teacher than learner. As it so often does, the Bible gives us some nitty-gritty principles to guide us.

Make Allowances for Your In-Laws. Learn to put up with a few differences.

Remember the Mercy God Has Shown You. When your in-laws offend you or just plain get on your nerves, make an effort to show mercy. Forgive them right away.

Clothe Yourselves with Love. In your relationship with your in-laws, let love be the guiding principle.

Maintaining appropriate boundaries is essential for any relationship to work. Those who struggle with overbearing or controlling in-laws can often benefit from good resources on Christian family relationships—or from Christian counseling. But all who desire the best for their families will practice Spirit-filled behavior, putting Christ and others first.

faith into action

Make a list of your in-laws' good points and share them with your spouse.

All intellectual improvement
arises from leisure.
—Samuel Johnson

To create is to cause to come into being. To re-create is to create anew. Recreation is renewal; it restores and refreshes.

Everyone needs times of recreation. Your future productivity depends on it. When work has no end, recreation has no beginning. And creativity is jeopardized.

Most of us know that we need recreation. We just have a hard time finding the time and energy. Recreation is a frame of mind as well as a physical activity. An afternoon at the lake can be wasted if your mental energies have not followed your body to the fishing spot. The object of recreation is to create

> It is good and proper for a man to eat and drink, and to find satisfaction in his toilsome labor.
> —Ecclesiastes 5:18

a fresh outlook on life and its related responsibilities.

Here are some tips for relaxing times of recreation. Seek:

- A change of scenery—get out of the house if possible.
- A different pace—if you sit a lot, do something active; if you're on your feet most of the time, find something that allows you to sit.
- A definite time—schedule a weekly day off and a quarterly getaway with your spouse. If you have a young family, have a weekly family night.
- A variety of options—rock climbing in the spring, bike trails for summer fun, apple orchard in the fall, or a toboggan run in the winter.

Recreation differs from vacation in that you can achieve recreation with a smaller investment of money and time. Every ministry couple needs a vacation, but they need many times of recreation.

faith into action

Schedule your next recreation activity today.

May we hold to that spirit, that we may be
as gentle and as kindly today as we were
on Christmas Eve, as generous tomorrow
as we were on Christmas morning.

—Peter Marshall

God appreciates celebration. He instituted annual feast days in the times of the Old Covenant. He commanded the Israelites to commemorate the rescue from Egypt with a feast. He sanctioned the marriage celebration in Galilee in the presence of Jesus. He gathers his angels to celebrate when a prodigal comes home. He is preparing the greatest celebration ever for his children in heaven.

Holidays are a way we can join in jubilation with the One who gives us all things to enjoy. Especially for families in ministry, holidays are significant occasions. Holidays often provide the opportunity for a trip. This enables the family to get away from the pressures of the church, and relax in a different setting. Since ministry involvement often places distance between relatives, holiday gatherings are a welcome time of reunion and togetherness.

Holidays remind us that there is more to life than deadlines, appointments, and challenges. They breathe a wisp of childlike glee into the soul and make even the return home seem pleasant. But ministers must allow the holidays to make as much of an impact on them as they make on the holiday!

faith into action

Check you calendar to ensure you've scheduled enough time off for holiday celebrations.

Sometimes the Lord rides out the storm
with us and other times He calms the
restless sea around us. Most of all, He
calms the storm inside us.

—Lloyd John Ogilvie

Perhaps no ministry-related concern is so often mentioned as the topic of stress. Its mushrooming force in the culture has been powerful. No person today is exempt from this predator. But it stalks those in ministry with particular vitriol.

Stress is the extreme pressure you feel when you're overwhelmed at the physical, emotional, and spiritual borders of your life. It's caused by tight schedules, sensory overload, dysfunctional relationships, financial deficits, health challenges, increased responsibilities, misplaced priorities, and more.

Stress introduces risk to your health, your relationships, and your work. Stress is a deadly foe. Okay. Been there. Done that. What's new? Formulate a personal strategy.

Manage Stress in Bite-Size Pieces. Too often we think the answer to stress is a vacation or sabbatical. Perhaps you need an extended absence to remedy your emotional exhaustion. But, unless you develop an ongoing plan to deal with it incrementally, you'll soon find yourself in the same predicament again.

Use the Stop Sign Method. On your way home, intentionally put ministry concerns out of your mind. Use a landmark, like a road sign, as your mental dumping point: "Beyond this point, I will resist thinking about ministry-related difficulties."

Build Emotional Nourishment into Your Weekly Routine. Set aside time to read books or articles that feed you, or listen to music that makes you feel alive and well.

Plan Mini Escapes. Do something you love and relish every minute of it. And remember God is your strength. He not only helps you with, he helps you through.

faith into action

Go to the library and check out a book for pure enjoyment.

> A person without a sense of humor is like a wagon without springs. It's jolted by every pebble on the road.
> —Henry Ward Beecher

Perhaps because of the serious nature of their calling; perhaps because of their often gregarious temperament; perhaps because . . . well, who knows why? Most people in ministry love to laugh! Assemble a group of preachers, teachers, or denominational leaders and humorous stories will roll right out of them. Laughter fills the room.

Humor is a God-given release valve for stress. It's healthy, not only for the mind and spirit, but for the body as well. People who laugh a lot are better adjusted and manage the bumps of life a little easier. Making humor a part of your life in ministry will be a valuable tool.

Not much is known about Jesus' temperament, but it is not difficult to imagine him delighting in the humorous things in life. Maybe he enjoyed sitting around the table at the home of Lazarus in Bethany, enjoying the amusement and company of friends. Maybe he traded practical jokes with his disciples as they made their journeys through the land of Israel. Though we do not often think of Christ in this way, surely the maker of joy and laughter would find pleasure in the simplicity of wholesome humor.

Be proactive in making humor a part of your life.

- Purchase some DVDs or downloads of Christian comedians and enjoy them with your spouse.
- Trade gentle practical jokes with your spouse on an ongoing basis.
- Invite some colleagues into your home who have a contagious sense of humor.

Be open to the humor of life—it's all around you; just look for it.

faith into action

Make your spouse laugh today.

Vacation is what you take when
you can't take what you've
been taking any longer.
—Author Unknown

The mountains? The beach? The lake? Where is your favorite
vacation spot?

Taking a vacation doesn't guarantee that your home will
be happy and healthy, but it does offer your family a number
of positive benefits.

- Stronger relationships—enjoying time together draws families
  closer.
- Enduring memories—photo albums, scrapbooks, and Web
  pages capture the moments that make a lasting imprint.

- Common identity—siblings can reminisce about good times and enjoy an instant, unique bond.
- Down time—there's no substitute for having time away from the stresses and frustrations of work life. It's good for your marriage and your kids.

Though it costs money, ministry families need to take their vacations away from home, if possible. There are too many distractions and urgent needs at home that prevent you from relaxing. Place a glass jar on the counter and invite the whole family to contribute to the vacation fund. Many banks offer a vacation club savings plan designed to help families put away funds for that special trip.

Vacations require planning. Start looking for ideas months in advance. Dream, research, and develop plans. Jesus knew the value of time away from the rigors of ministry. We should take the example and run with it—far outside the city limits.

faith into action

Make a list of vacation spots you'd like to visit in the next five years.

God is great, and therefore
He will be sought; He is good,
and therefore He will be found.

—Author Unknown

Personal quiet time with the Lord is your key to a balanced, tranquil life. George Muller warned: "It is a common temptation of Satan to make us give up the reading of the Word and prayer when our enjoyment is gone; as if it were of no use to read the Scriptures when we do not enjoy them, and as if it were no use to pray when we have no spirit of prayer."

It's not the lack of knowledge that makes it difficult. So what are the reasons?

- Lack of focus — letting other priorities take precedence.
- Incorrect perspective — seeing devotion as requirement rather than relationship.
- Sloppy schedule — late bedtimes and hurried mornings.
- Life seasons — unavoidable circumstances which warp your routine: motherhood, care-giving, extended illness.

Hurdling such obstacles and continuing to meet with God is absolutely essential. Devotion includes times of dialogue with God and an interest in his written Word. Relationships are that way. You like to discuss things with the one you love. Nobody makes you. Nobody punishes you if you don't. It's just a natural part of the relationship.

Prayer lists, journals, devotional guides — use whatever you need to focus on developing your spiritual life. But even more important is that you approach your devotional time with the anticipation of being with Someone whose presence you crave on a daily basis.

faith into action

Let the first thing you say as your feet hit the floor every morning be, "Good morning, Lord."

A healthy body is the guest-chamber
of the soul; to the sick, it's prison.
—Francis Bacon

People who exercise regularly generally have healthier bodies, more energy, and less disease. In fact, healthy bodies need exercise to maintain wellness. Exercise tones the muscles, lifts the spirit, strengthens the heart, and raises pain tolerance. It also relieves stress.

Squeezing exercise time into a full schedule can be a dilemma, though. If you and your spouse are empty-nesters, you can walk together in the evenings or take up a couples sport such as golf or tennis. If there are young children in the home, include your family in activities that promote exercise, such as hiking or biking on trails.

Many couples fall off the exercise wagon when bad weather comes or the cold season arrives. But you can exercise indoors too. Options such as walking in the mall, joining a fitness center, or using home workout videos may be the answer. Whatever you choose to do, it will take self-discipline to stay the course. Exercise is easy to neglect and, once neglected, hard to resume.

Physical fitness experts tell us to try for at least thirty minutes of exercise three times a week. Our bodies demand, "Just do something, besides sitting at the desk or riding in the car."

Though you might not have thought of it this way before, caring for your body is stewardship. Your body requires regular movement to be toned and healthy. We don't have the luxury of just doing what we want. The body, just like the soul, belongs to the Master. He wants us to glorify him with it.

In addition to keeping you in shape, exercise helps to relieve the stress of ministry. It just may lengthen your years of available for service to the Lord as well.

faith into action

Take a brisk walk with your spouse today.

Where shall my wondering soul begin? How shall I all to heaven aspire? A slave redeemed from death and sin, a brand plucked from eternal fire, how shall I equal triumphs raise, or sing my great Deliverer's praise?

—John Wesley

It won't win an academy award or an Olympic medal, but it elicits the Father's praise. Faithfulness is what heaven applauds. God likes finishers: those who stick with the task until they see it through. His kingdom is built by men and women who see beyond the humdrum of the daily routine and push steadily forward to the finished objective. In the parable of the talents, Jesus gave the highest praise to the servants who completed their assignments. He said, "Well done, good and faithful servant" (Matt. 25:21).

> Now it is required that those who have been given a trust must prove faithful.
> —1 Corinthians 4:2

You have been given a trust—a sacred assignment. The Master looked over the fields of harvest, provided you with the gifts you need to serve effectively, and gave you a task to complete. He simply asks that you stay on track and remain faithful.

Being faithful is simply stated, but it is not an easy task. You'll battle discouragement, boredom, frustration, and temptation. It's when you are tested that your resolve needs to bob to the surface like a small boat breaking a stormy wave. That's what it's all about—facing the storms of ministry and staying at the rudder.

The accolades of Hollywood glimmer for a brief evening filled with black ties and cocktail gowns; the prized commendation of the Heavenly Father will shine in the heart for eternity.

faith into action

Read Hebrews 11 and ponder what faithfulness means in your life.

The world appears very little
to a soul that contemplates
the greatness of God.

—Brother Lawrence

Stretched out by the constant tug of ministry demands? Someone once said, "Blessed are the flexible for they shall not be bent out of shape." Resilience is a very handy character trait for those in ministry. Some days, the elasticity of your spirit feels as if it's about to snap. It's at those times that you reach into the depths of your soul for strength to flex just a little more.

The palm trees of the tropics demonstrate a remarkable level of resilience. Gale force winds buffet them during the hurricane season. They bend crazily, their feathery fronds seeming to drag the earth. Yet when the skies clear and the debris is removed, the buoyant palm trees slide back up and resume their stately sentry duty.

We have witnessed the sad collapse of pastors who could not or would not bend. Maybe they were not adequately prepared for the demands of ministry. Maybe their natural dispositions thrust them toward this catastrophe. Maybe they were the victims of overwhelming circumstances. Whatever the reason, the results were tragic. Their emotional resources were depleted, their influences destroyed. And the kingdom lost more sentries.

It doesn't have to be this way. Christ's followers should be aware of their breaking point and be watchful for signs that they are nearing it. Then it is time to pull back and regroup. Those who accept the grace to bend will survive the storms without snapping.

faith into action

Ask your spouse to rate your degree of resilience.

Set yourself earnestly to see what
you are made to do, and then set
yourself earnestly to do it.
—Phillip Brooks

L eaders lead differently. It's supposed to be that way. God
has gifted each of those in ministry with certain strengths to
be used in his service. The variety of these gifts demonstrates
the genius of the divine Overseer of the church.

Oratory. Some have the gift of words. Whether from a
platform or on paper, they use their skill to communicate the
gospel of grace to others. These colorful leaders will be admired
for their brilliant rhetoric. While they may contribute to the
kingdom in many ways, their primary job is to articulate the
principles of the kingdom.

Administration. Some ministers can take utter chaos and organize it into a smooth system. Their talent in analyzing and addressing weaknesses is sometimes misunderstood, but they leave a trail of well-equipped, Christian fellowships behind them. They promote the kingdom through memos and paintbrushes.

Vision. Some who minister are dreamers. They can sketch the future in dazzling hues, drawing their followers with them as they recognize the potential laid out before them. These leaders help people to hope again.

Nurture. Then there are those who are skilled in developing the gifts of others. Their eyes can see the embryonic talents in Christ's followers. Their hearts are geared to the task of mentoring. Wherever they go, they build up the kingdom by investing in others.

In reality, most leaders have a combination of the above gifts, some are stronger in one area, some are stronger in another. Have you discovered your ministry gift? It's not far away—maybe as close as your hands—and as dear as your heart.

faith into action

Help your spouse determine what his or her greatest ministry gift is.

His forever, only His! Who the
Lord and me shall part? Ah, with
what a rest of bliss Christ can
fill the loving heart!
—George W. Robinson

Does your life in ministry look like you thought it would when you started? Many who are involved in kingdom service look at what's behind them and what's before them and scratch their heads. It wasn't supposed to be quite like this.

Despite your commitment and the blessings of God, life is a winding path that doesn't conform to the map of your youthful ambitions. It doesn't mean that God has failed or that your plans were too lofty. God's pattern is sometimes obscured by the peripheral details of life. He is still bringing to pass his good will in your personal life and ministry.

> He who began a good work in you will carry it on to completion until the day of Jesus Christ.
>
> —Philippians 1:6

Encountering detours and construction zones in your ministry is not an indication that you've chosen the wrong path. Neither youthful vision nor mature reflection can predict how God might use such experiences to work his plan, but experience and church history show that he does. His grace will carry you through, and when he has completed his work, you'll be astounded at what eternity reveals.

Your perspective of progress may be a little cloudy right now. Relationship challenges and ministry difficulties often loom so large that it's hard to see what's beyond them. Never assess your path when you're in a pothole. Hold onto the fact that obedience and faithfulness will be rewarded, if not in time, in eternity.

faith into action

Write a brief paragraph in a journal or notebook about someone whose life has been changed as a result of your ministry.

I am restless, but with you there is peace;
in me there is bitterness, but with you
there is patience; I do not understand your
ways, but you know the way for me.

—Dietrich Bonheoffer

Bitterness is a formidable foe. The very sound of the word makes you want to draw back. Bitter means a wry taste, a lack of sweetness, a shriveled deadness. Because of its subtlety, bitterness is especially dangerous. Like a soundless serpent it lays in wait, winding closer with each disappointment and every injustice. It bides its time, waiting for exhaustion and discouragement to weaken its prey, stalking in the shadows.

Anger flares instantly. Frustration bursts out. But bitterness creeps slowly around the soul. How can you protect yourself from the danger of bitterness?

Look for Its Scent. Examine your heart regularly before the Lord to detect the early warnings of a sour attitude.

Recognize Its Signs. Bitterness often shows itself in a tendency toward criticism of others or frequent sarcasm about ministry.

Reject Its Seduction. When bitterness shows it's fangs, immerse yourself in the sweetness of God's promises.

Those who become careless and fall prey to bitterness lose so much. The kingdom suffers, and those who watch the tragedy can be devoured as well. Sin is cruel. Satan is ruthless. The culture is godless. Even the church world is often heartless.

But Christ is faultless. His power within enables his ministers to stand in the rubble of life and remain steadfast in soul and tender in heart. Bitterness must bow to grace.

faith into action

When you're tempted to be critical today, examine your motive.

Never give in. Never give in. Never, never, never, never—in nothing, great or small, large or petty. Never give in except to conviction of honor and good sense.

—Winston Churchill

Diligence is the foundation of successful ministry.

No one ever accomplished his or her goals on talent and opportunity alone. To finish the course and keep the faith requires the unrelenting resolve of diligence. Those who practice diligence always try again, always get back up again, and always reach out again.

Diligence Is the Parent of Creativity. Diligent leaders see the obstacles, and don't give up until they find a solution. People that exercise diligence know that the conditions of a situation aren't as crucial as the determination to overcome.

> We want each of you to show this same diligence to the very end.
> —Hebrews 6:11

Diligence Requires Consistent Performance. The path to eternal inheritance lies in performing consistently on a daily basis. There are no back doors to spiritual triumph, either in private devotion or in matters of ministry. Ordinary moments infused with diligence create the momentum that accomplishes what others thought impossible.

Diligence Requires Focus. Remember that today's headline is not the final draft of history. Rumors echo, emotions fluctuate, and people move on. Amidst the chaos, diligent leaders continue to minister because the tale is still unfolding; the exclamation point goes at the end, not halfway through. Those in ministry have no time to worry about crafting their legacy; they are too busy being diligent in matters that advance the mission.

Diligence Births Victory. William Penn said, "Patience and diligence, like faith, remove mountains." Ministry is all about mountain-moving; the diligent see the rocks crumble.

faith into action

Look up *diligence* in the dictionary and claim one definition as your mantra for the week.

More about Jesus would I know, more
of His grace to others show.

—Eliza E. Hewitt

Compassion is the twin sister of charity. You rarely see one without the other. In ministry, compassion is standard equipment. Because your ministry is wrapped up in the heart of God, who is deeply touched by the pain of people, it's almost impossible to minister effectively without feeling the throb of compassion in your soul.

Scripture tells us to clothe ourselves with compassion. This denotes a purposeful action, putting on the work clothes of kindness—as an act of the will. Compassion doesn't happen automatically. While some temperaments are naturally more sensitive than others, every person can choose the garment of compassion as part of his or her daily dress.

Compassion is not quick and easy clichés or insincere offers. Compassion is:

Tapping Into the Heart of God. He loves people so much he did something about it.

Choosing to Make Another's Pain Your Own. Make the effort to get inside their pain so you can understand it.

Living with a Vulnerable Heart. Maintain awareness of the wounds of the ones you serve.

Compassion is the precursor to serving in a spirit of holiness. When we are moved with compassion for those around us, our ministry will propel us forward to touch their lives.

As compassion is essential in professional ministry, so it is essential between husband and wife. Let no one be more sensitive, understanding, or caring toward your spouse than you. Not that you would discourage others from being compassionate, but that you would demonstrate to your spouse that no one cares for him or her more than you.

faith into action

Plan a specific act of compassion and carry it out.

Take the first walk with God! Let Him
go forth with thee; by streams, or
sea, or mountain path, seek still
His company.
—Horatius Bonar

Thomas Kinkade has built his iconic art career on the themes of light and home: glowing cottages, shimmering city streets, glittering windows, beaming lighthouses. To view one of his masterful renditions is to sense tranquility and peace.

Peace appeals to everyone, whether they admit it or not. We were designed for peace. God did not create his human image-bearers to be perpetrators of conflict, to be savage in nature and action. He created us to desire peace and harmony. Even our own bodies teach us this. Stress makes the heart beat faster, the blood pressure rise, and the emotions intensify.

Let the peace
of Christ rule in
your hearts.
—Colossians 3:15

Adrenalin helps us meet a crisis, but a constant supply of it will exhaust our energy. The body was designed to enjoy peace.

Peace is a universal desire. Warring nations may relish the thought of conquering one another, but they take little pleasure in the chaos, uncertainty, and loss associated with battle. Battle is to be endured until soldiers experience reprieve around the cooking stove. Peace is the object of nations. Peace is the goal of administrations. Peace, however elusive, is still an enviable prize no where more than in the home of a ministry couple.

Peace is essential in your ministry—in the heart, in the soul, in the home, in the church. Let it rule; give it the go ahead to be supreme. The wording in Colossians 3:15 suggests that we should let the peace of God act as our umpire. Behind every decision or every action, the peace of God should be working as the motivator—that inner calm that guides those who let him be the Lord.

faith into action

Learn what kinds of activities create and sustain peace within your partner's heart and soul. Make plans to bring more of that kind of activity into your family life.

God moves in a mysterious way His wonders to perform; He plants His footsteps in the sea and rides upon the storm.
—William Cowper

History is God's PowerPoint presentation. It reveals the variety of media through which he demonstrates his power.

Through Miraculous Acts. In the Old Testament, God revealed his awesome strength through the things he did. He formed the world. He caused the flood. He split the Red Sea. He distributed manna. He tumbled Jericho's walls. He withheld rain. He burned the sacrifice. He won Gideon's battle. He stopped the lions. He walked in the furnace. Over and over he gave his people visual demonstrations of his might.

> I have seen you in the sanctuary and beheld your power and your glory.
> —Psalm 63:2

Through the Cycles of Nature. Through nature, God continues to show his power. He monitors earthquakes, allows hurricanes and tornadoes, creates the eclipse, ignites lightening, produces thunder, sends the rain and snow, changes the seasons, and polishes the sun's morning glow.

Through Prophecy and Promises. A promise kept is a sign of strength. Throughout history, God has left a trail of fulfilled predictions, revealing his vast resources to his people. By causing them to come true, he demonstrated that he is powerful enough to do what he says. When his promises prove true in the lives of believers, his name is glorified.

Through Transformed People. Over and over again, God reveals his power by transforming the hearts and lives of his people by his grace. He allows them to be tested, puts them under scrutiny, and dazzles the world when his power is revealed in fragile humanity.

You have the opportunity to display God's powerful work too. Cooperate with the Holy Spirit to bring about the changes that would allow God's power and majesty to shine even more brightly in your life.

faith into action

Reflect on a powerful act of God you experienced today.

Coming together is a beginning.
Keeping together is progress.
Working together is success.
—Henry Ford

Think about the teamwork required to build a high-rise building. Starting with the foundation, workers lay beams, pour concrete, and weld seams until a mammoth skeleton takes shape. Slowly, it mushrooms upward. Fiberglass and sheetrock are added. Windows are placed; elevators installed; offices furnished. The structure towers over the skyline, a monument to cooperation.

The apostle Paul says the work of the kingdom is like that. As leaders, it is your job to oversee the plans, guide the workers, settle disputes, and ensure the project follows the blueprint.

Encouraging cooperation is the way to build efficiently.

Cooperation in a ministry setting has challenges. Counteract them.

> In him the whole building is joined together and rises to become a holy temple in the Lord.
> —Ephesians 2:21

Project a Positive Attitude. This outlook is contagious.

Listen to Others' Opinions. Giving others a voice secures their buy-in and strengthens your plan.

Accept Advice. Model for your followers that everyone can benefit from counsel.

Maintain Proper Perspective. How you work together is often as important as what you accomplish.

For ministry couples, healthy cooperation at home is the foundation for healthy cooperation in ministry. Work with your spouse as a team. As you do, not only will you gain practical experience and learning that you can share with your ministry teams at church, you'll also learn to respect and admire one another at an even deeper level.

faith into action

Commend those under you for their recent efforts in the ministry.

Take my will and make it Thine—
it shall be no longer mine; take
my heart it is Thine own; it
shall be Thy royal throne.
—Frances R. Havergal

If ministry were a highway, transition would be the bridge. Sometimes you see the bridge well in advance. Other times, it sneaks up on you.

No two pastoral transitions are alike but, there are certain things you can expect during any transition:

- Conflicting emotions—leaving brings sadness; yet new opportunities promise excitement and enthusiasm.
- Lame duck syndrome—once people know you're leaving, leadership is more challenging.

> Commit to the LORD whatever you do, and your plans will succeed.
> —Proverbs 16:3

- Changing relationships—people begin to detach emotionally to protect themselves from the loss they're about to experience.
- Increased strain at home—moving is just plain stressful. Whether across town or to a different state, when there are boxes everywhere, the whole family is more irritable.
- Financial strain—moving always costs more than you think it will.
- Exhaustion—between the packing, the cleaning, and the emotional drain, you may be surprised by how fatigued you feel on the other side of the move.

Transition can be scary. But as you stand with your spouse and look across the chasm to the other side, you know that your transition means progress. Remember that you can count on God being with you every step. He's promised that your plans will succeed if you commit them to him.

faith into action

Talk with your spouse about what is most stressful for each of you in thinking about a transition.

For information on seminars, scheduling
speaking engagements, or to contact the authors:

Stan and Linda Toler
PO Box 892170
Oklahoma City, OK 73189-2170
www.stantoler.com